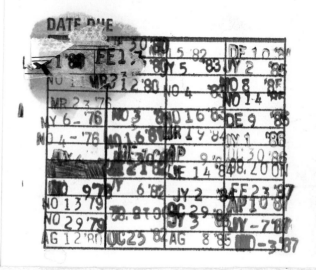

The Future of Federalism

THE GODKIN LECTURES
AT HARVARD UNIVERSITY
1962

*The Godkin Lectures on the Essentials
of Free Government and the Duties of the
Citizen were established at Harvard University
in memory of Edwin Lawrence Godkin (1831–1902).*

THE
FUTURE
OF
FEDERALISM

Nelson A. Rockefeller

HARVARD
UNIVERSITY
PRESS

CAMBRIDGE

1962

Second printing

Contents

I.   FREEDOM AND FEDERALISM   1

II. FEDERALISM AND NATIONAL LIFE   29

III. FEDERALISM AND FREE WORLD
     ORDER   59

*These lectures were delivered on the evenings of
February 7, February 8, and February 9, 1962.*

The Future of Federalism

I

Freedom and Federalism

In the ominous spring of 1939, a bright and sunny May 3rd was a day marked by Adolf Hitler with another bellicose speech to the Reichstag calling for a showdown on Poland. On the same day, the League of Nations opened its "peace pavilion" at the World's Fair in New York City. And also on this same day, which seems so remote from the present instant, there was published a vigorous critique of American political life by a visitor from abroad, famed in intellectual and academic circles, who had just delivered a series of lectures on the American presidency. The visitor was Harold J. Laski. And the obituary he wrote upon an historic American political doctrine bore the title: "The Obsolescence of Federalism."

How did Professor Laski conclude that the age of federalism was languishing near death?

He did concede that "federalism is the appropriate governmental technique for an expanding capitalism." But, he declaimed, a "contracting capitalism cannot afford the luxury of federalism." Leaping from this premise, he insisted that the failure of the federal idea was unmistakably plain not only in the United States but also elsewhere in the world—in Canada, Australia, Germany. And he explained this universal failure in these words: "Whether we take the conditions of labor, the level of taxation, the standards of education, or the supply of amenities like housing and recreation, it has become clear that the true source of decision is no longer at the circumference, but at the center, of the state. For 48 separate units to seek to compete with the integrated power of giant capitalism is to invite defeat in almost every element of social life where approximate uniformity of condition is the test of the good life." in the

~~The two~~ decades since have dealt a harsh retort to Professor Laski's pronouncement on federalism in the United States. It has been proven wrong in economic, social, and political terms.

In the first place, the American free economy has not contracted but has continued its dynamic expansion. Private enterprise has become more vigorous, more creative—and better able to bring to the American workingman and woman the highest standard of living ever known by any nation, any time, anywhere in history. The power of the people over the functioning of the economy, all this while, has been maintained and even extended. A great array of political and economic devices—the income tax, inheritance laws, antitrust statutes, new and diversified mechanisms for capital accumulation, and the revolution in science—has assured that "giant capitalism," far from becoming more "integrated," has become more decentralized.

The grim prognosis of 50 years ago has also been proven wrong in strictly political terms. For federalism—its ideas and its practice—has continued to show itself the adaptable and creative form of self-government that the Founding Fathers of this nation conceived it to be. Decisions vital to national well-being have increasingly been made at the "circumference"—the states—as well as at the national "center," of political power.

These lectures are dedicated to the conviction that these basic political, social, and economic facts of life—and the lessons they carry for us—are crucial to the whole fate of freedom and of free men everywhere in this mid-twentieth century.

I do not use the word "freedom" casually. For nothing less than the historic concept of the free individual's worth and dignity, defined and attested by the whole Judeo-Christian tradition, is at stake in our world. Nor do I mention this nation's Founding Fathers from mere historic sentimentalism. The basic belief that these lectures will finally state is the urgent, historic necessity summoning Americans of this generation to match the founders of this nation in their political creativity, boldness, and vision.

The Founding Fathers devised a structure of order for a nation within which free men could work and prosper in peace. We are required to help build such a framework for freedom not merely for a nation but for the free world of which we are an integral part. And we are called to do this with far greater speed, I believe, than many of us realize or admit.

Ultimately, the great part of our debt to the past may lie in this fact: the federal idea, so basic to both personal freedom and national unity in the history of America, can now be extended and applied to bring order, strength, and progress to the world of free peoples.

———

Let us look, first, at the federal concept and its evolution in our nation. Let us examine some of its practical applications on working levels of national, state, and local government. Let us observe its capacity for adaptation and change, over the decades. Let us see its critical relevance and relation to a free economy—and a pluralistic society. Let us always remember, however, that the *supreme* issue before us through all the inquiry is this: how to make freedom itself work and endure in the world today.

I am sure you are not surprised that a governor of a large state in our federal union elects to speak of the federal idea of political life. The concept is associated in all our minds with the rights and powers of the individual states. Yet, my own political experience began in appointive posts at the national level under three different Presidents.

In 1940—more than two decades ago—I went to Washington. After mingled accomplishment and frustration in various appointive posts over a period of 16 years, I turned to elective public office on the state level—and ran for Governor of New York in 1958. I made this choice on the basis of my recognition that the critical political decisions in government are, and must be, primarily shaped and made by elected officials—or, as my Latin-American friends would say, by "the authentic representatives of the people."

It is with this particular perspective on our

democratic processes that I underline my deep
personal conviction that the future of freedom
lies in the federal idea.

The Federal Idea

The federal idea: what does this mean?

Let me first make it clear that I do not speak of
the federal idea as merely a mechanical or technical or abstract formula for government operations. I refer to the federal idea broadly as a concept of government by which a sovereign people,
for their greater progress and protection, yield a
portion of their sovereignty to a political system
that has more than one center of sovereign power,
energy, and creativity. No one of these centers or
levels has the power to destroy another. Under the
Constitution, for example, there are two principal
centers of government power—state and federal.
As a practical matter, local government, by delegation of state authority under the principle of
"home rule," is a third such key center of power.
The federal idea, then, is above all an idea of a
shared sovereignty at all times responsive to the
needs and will of the people in whom sovereignty
ultimately resides.

Our federal idea is complex and subtle. It involves a balance of strengths. It puts into play a
sharing of powers not only among different levels

of government but—on each level—a separation of powers between the legislative, executive, and judicial branches of government. And it clearly signifies more than mere governmental structure. It demands faith in—and an environment for— the free play of individual initiative, private enterprise, social institutions, political organizations, and voluntary associations—all operating within a framework of laws and principles affirming the dignity and freedom of man.

A federal system, then, seeks stability without rigidity, security without inertia. It encourages innovation and inventiveness—governed by principle, and guided by purpose. It assures responsiveness more thoughtful than mere reflex—and liberty that does not lapse toward anarchy. In short, it seeks to hold the delicately precarious balance between freedom and order upon which depend decisively the liberty, peace, and prosperity of the individual.

A more full and meaningful "definition" of the federal idea may be offered in the form of what I believe are four of the critical ways in which the federal concept operates.

First: The federal idea fosters diversity within unity. In this land that reaches from ocean to ocean, the great social, economic, and political problems vary profoundly as they may appear, for example,

before the people of Wyoming, the people of
Louisiana, or the people of Massachusetts. In
meeting many of these problems, a sweeping gen-
eralized edict from the national government
might well be futile or even fatuous. Yet, in our
federal concept, the national government is called
upon to work with state governments in ways
encouraging the states more effectively to resolve
their own problems in their own way.

The simplest technical illustration of this practice is the granting of federal aid to the states,
which has two key purposes. It stimulates the
states to action—and to higher standards of action
—by offering matching funds on specific conditions. And it also strives to equalize opportunities
for the citizens of states with unequal resources.
Thus, in terms of the federal tax-dollar, a state
like New York "pays out" $3 for every $1 of federal aid returned, while a state like Arkansas gives
$1 and receives back more than $2.50. By all such
devices, the federal concept recognizes diversity
—and achives unity.

Second: The federal idea permits and encourages creativity, imagination, and innovation in
meeting the needs of the people. Those needs, if
not met by private action, can be met at the local,
the state, or the national level of government.

By providing several sources of political strength and creativity, a federal system invites inventive leadership—on all levels—to work toward genuine solutions to the problems of a diverse and complex society. These problems—whether they concern civil rights or urban development, industrialization or automation, natural resources or transportation—never arise at the same instant and in the same way throughout a great nation. A federal system, however, allows these problems to be met at the time and in the area where they first arise. If local solutions are not forthcoming, it is still possible to bring to bear the influence, the power, and the leadership of either the state or the national government.

Third: The federal idea is a pluralistic idea. It gives scope to many energies, many beliefs, many initiatives, and enlists them for the welfare of the people. It encourages diversity of thought, of culture, and of beliefs. It gives unparalleled opportunity for the development of private institutions —social, political and economic.

Whereas a tightly centralized government tends, by its disproportionate weight and power, to stifle diversity and creativity in both the public and private sectors, a federal system provides room for both infinite variety and creativity in all sectors of national life. This is equally true for political organizations, philanthropic associations, social institutions, or economic enterprises.

Fourth: The federal idea is characterized by a balance which prevents excesses and invites the full, free play of innovation and initiative. This balance is essentially achieved by: the division of powers between the national and state governments, the separation of legislative, executive, and judicial authority, the absence of monolithic national parties, the permissive encouragement given to local municipal governments to achieve a measure of home rule either in fact or in law, the competitive action of commercial enterprise, and—above all—the freedom of individual initiative, rooted in a basic and unwavering belief in the dignity of the human person.

———

Let me now meet here an obvious challenge on the question of the balance within the American federal system. This is the assertion that the most dynamic forces in our society—social and economic needs, technological evolution, national peril, and governmental complexity—all conspire to decree a pitiless growth in the centralization of political authority, whether we wish it or not. The massive pressures of the Great Depression and of

World War II (so it has been argued) made a bloat-
ing of central government inevitable. And hence
state and local governments supposedly must with-
draw from the arenas of great political, economic,
and social decision.

The Growth of Government

As the demands of society have increased, the
national government has, indeed, not only become
larger but also has become more deeply involved
in state and local affairs. But, the striking fact in
our domestic political experience since World
War II has not been the growth of federal government—but the far more rapid expansion of state
and local government, to meet growing social
needs.

With the resources and attention of the federal
government increasingly devoted to defense, foreign aid, and international relations, the rising
pressures to meet domestic needs have been directed more and more to state and local government.

It is true that, from 1950 through 1960, total
national expenditures moved from 40.3 billion to
77.2 billion a 92 per cent increase in a decade.
We must note, however, that practically all of this
increase was allotted directly to the Defense Department. If we subtract the expenditures of the

Defense Department, national expenditures increased only 24 per cent—from 27.1 billion to 33.5 billion. And included in these figures are huge sums for activities clearly tied to the defense effort—the Atomic Energy Commission, veterans' affairs, and mutual security. Considering the increased cost of goods and services in the fifties, there was only a modest increase in nondefense expenditures at the national level during the decade.

In the same period, total *state* expenditures jumped from 13.2 billion to 32.5 billion—an increase of 146 per cent. Allowing for large population increases, this meant a leap from $89 per capita in 1950 to $182 per capita in 1960. Expenditures at the local level are equally impressive. In cities over 25,000, for example, the outlay went from 4.9 billion in 1950 to 12.3 billion in 1960, a staggering jump of 150 per cent.

If we recall again the dismal prognosis offered on the future of federalism more than 20 years ago, we are tempted to ask: if this be "obsolescence," what, then, would be the size of growth?

The Role of the States

I offer further proof by referring simply to the magnitude of certain programs of the government of the State of New York—and their comparative relation to matching efforts by the government of the United States:

In education: State aid to elementary and secondary education in the State of New York totaled $753 million in the 1961–1962 fiscal year, or $87 million more than the President requested of the Congress for the whole nation in 1961 (and, as you know, what was requested on the national level far surpassed what was appropriated).

In civil defense: the $100 million for the New York program, made law in the special session of the State Legislature in the fall of 1961, is equivalent to approximately one-third of the program enacted in Washington the same year for the entire nation.

In power development: The State Power Authority of New York has built more hydroelectric generating capacity on the Niagara and St. Lawrence rivers in the past ten years, with the funds of private bondholders, than all the hydroelectric dams of the TVA system.

In housing: While the federal housing program enacted by the Congress last year authorized the sum of $5 billion, I recently proposed a New York State housing program which for New York City alone would involve the identical sum of $5 billion—these funds to be supplied through the newly created State Housing Finance Agency at no cost to the taxpayers.

I do not cite these facts and figures to imply that state and national governments are pitted against one another—locked in some bizarre contest to surpass one another in size and expenditure. Nothing could be further from the true relation of complementing and cooperating that must mark a healthy federalism. Yet these statistics do suggest that the role of the state, within American federalism, is far from "obsolete." It is as dynamic and promising as is the federal idea itself.

Something more than arithmetic attests the unique role of the state. It is dramatized by the whole sweep of our modern social history. Erroneously, this history has come to be exclusively associated, in the mind of a generation, with the New Deal. The historical fact is, of course, that the New Deal did face and meet deep crises in our society, did institute vital social reforms and economic regulations, and did take the force out of stresses that could have resulted in conflict and catastrophe for the nation.

Yet—while the New Deal accomplished these major social advances and did much to restore the confidence of the people—its leaders did not display great comprehension of the nature and workings of our economic system. They showed little or no awareness of the need to create a climate for growth to encourage an expanding American economy, vital to the achievement of full employment, social objectives, and the self-realization of the individual. For all the New Deal's conscientious concern for human values, it took the advent of World War II to dispose of the problems of depression and unemployment.

This experience brought home the fact that it does not suffice to understand social needs and aspirations—without also fully understanding the dynamics of our economic system.

The Roots of Social Reform

A still more striking—and overlooked—fact about the New Deal is that its major and most successful actions in social reform had been anticipated, by experiment and practice, on the state level or by private institutions.

The history of the years before 1932 tells this story plainly. Time and again, states like Massachusetts, Wisconsin, or New York acted on their own initiative to protect the health, safety, and welfare of the individual, while guarding his rights and broadening his opportunities in the nation's free economy. This was true of factory inspection or the limitation of hours of labor. It was true of child labor or women's labor. It was true of unemployment compensation and social security.* In all such cases, the ferment of ideas and innovations worked its way *up* through the federal system—often from private initiative.

It is also important to note, too, that those elements of the New Deal which failed were largely in areas *not* tested by prior experience at the state level. These included such major economic regulatory actions as the National Recovery Administration, the Agricultural Adjustment Act, and other actions based on an economy of scarcity and on the restriction of competition and production. These were examples of action by centralized government which proved counterproductive to the goal of full employment. They turned out to be deterrents to economic growth.

This parenthesis on the impact of the New Deal only serves to make still clearer the practical workings—and ultimate implications—of the federal idea. This idea deeply involves the whole political, cultural, social, and economic environment— just as it reflects a great part of our history as a nation. And while this idea implies limits and

* Factory inspection, Massachusetts, 1879; old age pensions, Alaska, 1915; child labor, Massachusetts, 1842; women's hour laws, 42 states by 1933; unemployment insurance began with private plans but reached fruition in Wisconsin Unemployment Compensation Act of 1932.

checks against excessive power, its living purpose and intent are *creative* and *affirmative*. It is not a theoretical device to narrow or constrict political action. It is a way to amplify it.

The federal idea is not an excuse for keeping necessary things from being done. It is almost the exact opposite—a flexible and imaginative device to open not one but many avenues of political action for economic and social progress.

The essential supremacy of the people through their exercise of political power is, above all, vital to the life of the federal idea.

So close to the people, so interwoven with their deepest beliefs and their daily lives, is the federal concept that this concept is, in fact, conceivable and workable only when the people act as responsible individuals—as concerned citizens—and not merely as members of an economic class, ethnic group, religious faith, occupational calling, or private organization. The working of the federal idea, in short, depends upon the *whole* political environment, the full intellectual climate, the sum of the spirit and purposes of all citizenry, and their individual and collective sense of responsibility. This responsibility—I believe deeply— means political participation, not merely in voting, but in active working for one's party and in standing for public office.

My own decision to run for governor in 1958 was firmly grounded in this belief. I promptly received much contrary advice. "Don't get into politics," I was told repeatedly. "Politics is a dirty business." My reply to those who gave me this advice was simply this: "Politics is the life blood of democracy. To call politics 'dirty' is to call democracy 'dirty.'"

The truth is that anyone in a democratic society who believes that his political environment has become "dirty," and therefore scornfully turns his back on it, has become, in effect, a political refugee in his own society. Politics, of course, requires sweat, work, combat, and organization. But these should not be ugly words for any free people.

"Organization" in politics, for example, is not a sign of some sordid tyranny. It is what makes democracy itself function. And its roots must strike far beneath the surface of national, state, or community government. It must draw its strength and vitality from the people—through the ward leaders, the precinct chiefs, the block captains.

No concept of government, not even the lofty and rich promise of the federal idea itself, can truly work except as dedicated men and women in these positions, men and women in the tens of thousands, make it work. Grand ideas of government—lofty abstract principles, even the wisest constitutions and laws—depend for their very life and meaning on the willingness of citizens and leaders to apply them and to improve them.

What factors, then, tend to impair—in political practice—the effectiveness of our federal system in theory?

In the political environment of today, I would mark three pervasive attitudes or tendencies as plainly damaging to our processes of government. The first is the scorn or scepticism toward practical, partisan politics that I have already mentioned. The second is an addiction to political labels and slogans, along lines loosely called "liberal" and "conservative." The third is a timidity of leadership that rarely glimpses the dawn of any new concepts—but passively awaits the high noon of crisis.

Political Aloofness

The aversion to the "rough-and-tumble," the public exposure, of partisan political life has choked off a vast amount of civic energy and creativity, precisely at the time in our history when such energy and creativity are most urgently needed. And the sources of this aversion go beyond the shallow attitude that shuns politics as "dirty."

For a whole generation, now, this withdrawal has tended to be rationalized as something wise and discriminating. A great part of our youth has grown up to believe that political parties are cheap and shoddy instruments, that political life is either comic or corrupt, and that partisanship itself must be intellectually suspect. The fashion, in all this, has been to exalt the calm and detached surveyor of the cluttered political scene, untroubled by the noisy turmoil beneath him, serene upon his pinnacle of self-appreciation, uncontaminated by the touch of reality.

I am not criticizing *active* intellectual independence or political mobility. Freedom—and freshness—of political judgment are essential to the vitality of our two-party system. The voter who splits his ticket—or who changes parties when he feels the candidates or the issues warrant it— is *adding* to the responsiveness and responsibility of *both* national parties.

But I do criticize political aloofness—based merely upon an overly fastidious distaste for partisanship itself. This I deeply deplore. It is foolish, because it ignores the very nature of a democratic process that depends upon active, intelligent, aggressive partisanship for its very life. And it is reckless, because the level of this real-life combat—the constructiveness of political debate and the rationality of political argument—cannot be improved by persuading a free people to declare themselves, politically, a nation of conscientious objectors.

No democracy, in short, can afford to view the political scene as a kind of spectator sport, played for the amusement of the detached observers. The truth is that our democracy needs to sharpen the debate between parties and within the parties. And this need is denied or evaded by a condescension and contempt for the political life, a muting of voices, a preference for smug silence.

Political Labels

A second distortion of political reality can be equally damaging. This is the obsession with political labels which results in the rigid classification of laws, leaders, and policies as "liberal" or "conservative." We all know that, in any serious historical sense, these terms have lost all meaning. The use of such artificial labels, in political debate, merely distorts the issue and confuses the citizen. It substitutes the slogan for thought, the false label for the serious goal. It invites the citizen, in effect, to say: "Don't confuse me with the facts. I've already made up my mind."

The confusion caused by such labels can be

quickly seen if we note, for example, the policies and actions essential to accelerated economic growth—which is basic to all our major objectives as a people today. Under the now-meaningless terms of "liberal" and "conservative," some would hold that economic policies welcomed by labor are "liberal," while those cheered by business are "conservative." Yet *all* progress for *all* sections of the community depends upon interrelated factors of economic growth.

A prospering business depends upon a favorable economic climate. Labor depends upon the jobs that only a prospering business can provide. Business depends upon a responsible and prospering labor force. Both need the productive genius of agriculture. And all the social services of the government depend for their financing upon revenues attainable only through general economic progress and growth.

This is the *dynamic circle* of progress for our free society. It must not be broken by false issues, imaginary conflicts, or false labels. And it can be forged only by the kind of political leadership that looks, realistically and steadfastly, to the general good of all the people.

To illustrate specifically from personal experience . . . When I took office as governor, there were 600,000 unemployed in the State of New

York. Business had been leaving the state because of an unfavorable economic climate. And the outgoing administration left, as its fiscal heritage, budget requests calling for expenditures of $2.3 billion, backed by revenue of only $1.6 billion— a deficit of $700 million.

To restore the state's fiscal integrity required cutting expenditures, instituting economies, and raising taxes. None of these moves was popular, I can assure you. But the restoration of confidence in the state was fundamental to improving the climate for economic growth. And it set us on the road to expanding business and industry, rising employment, declining unemployment, and a far greater capacity to meet our social responsibilities as a state. As an example of this capacity, the state this year is providing $500 million more for education than when I took office—in other words, a 90 per cent increase in state aid to education in just four years.

Where—in all this brief history—does a policy or an act become "liberal" or "conservative"? According to these labels, action to improve the business climate is "conservative," and increased aid to education is "liberal." The fact is that the implied distinction is false and deceiving.

If an action clearly serves the public good, what responsible leader will refrain from it for fear of the label it may bear? And if the action bring harm to the common weal, no label—or slogan—can make it right.

Political Leadership

The power of the federal idea rests, in important part, upon the opportunity it gives for action. We have noted some of the ways in which this power and opportunity may be limited, in real life. Yet the truth is that there may be no limitation upon leadership of any kind so severe as the simple un-willingness to lead.

In concrete terms: if a state government lacks the political courage to meet the needs of its people by using its own taxing power—if it prefers to escape by letting the national government do the taxing and then return the money to the state— the leadership of this state puts itself in an exceed-ingly poor position to weep over the growth of federal power. The preservation of states' *rights* —in short— depends upon the exercise of states' *responsibilities*.

The key to this exercise, obviously, is responsi-ble leadership in the executive and legislative branches of government. Here—as with federalism itself—we cannot seize some simplified definition to explain the matter. The quality of leadership is a many-faceted thing—subtle in the kind of strength that prudently falls short of the arbitrary or the authoritarian. But I think that this leadership has one most clear sign and expression. It must have the vision to foresee and the courage to meet problems and challenges before they grow to the ugly size of crises—by which time even the most detached or unperceptive public opinion clamors for action.

We live in an age that, by its very pace of change, severely tests all capacity for such leadership. The challenges themselves come large, and they surge swiftly. In higher education, for example, and in New York State alone, a survey of coming needs based on existing school enrollments has shown that we must double the total of all existing facilities in the next 10 years—and triple them in 25 years. Full public awareness of such accelerating needs almost surely must lag behind the facts.

In such a time of rapid change, timidity in government only compounds the problems. One is reminded, here, of the French premier who said sardonically: "The art of politics lies not in finding solutions to fundamental problems, but in keeping quiet those who raise them." To anyone who might be tempted to live by this formula in politics, I can only say that it offers a possible prescription for the tragedy that befell France 20 years ago. Surely we can find happier models for our American destiny.

Yet few things may trouble this destiny so much as a political disposition to confuse the *leading* of public opinion with the *reflecting* of it. We have all witnessed, in recent years, the widening temptation to hinge political judgment on the techniques of marketing research—the polls and surveys supposedly measuring the public temper. There exist, today, some 40 or 50 firms operating on the national level to tell political leaders and groups how the public is reacting and what it would most like to hear. Any leadership that is merely a creature of such devices is not even playing politics. It is merely caught in the complex conjuring act of a ventriloquist.

I do not believe for an instant, either, that the public, in our democracy, wants any such passive and acquiescent leadership. It does not turn to leadership as to a mirror, to study its own reflection. It looks for something very different: a definition of, and a dedication to, those principles and policies which enable a free people to grow, to prosper, and to extend its own horizon of hope.

I doubt if any democracy, without such vision

and courage, without such leadership, can seriously expect to survive the mortal trials of our century.

Let me summarize briefly:

The historic application of the federal idea—reconciling unity and diversity—is probably the supreme American contribution to the struggle of all self-governing peoples to build political structures strong enough to assure freedom and order in their lives.

Our own federal system provides a unique arena for imaginative and inventive action and leadership, responsive and responsible to the people.

The practical fulfillment of this promise in our political heritage depends critically, however, upon the health of the national economy, the momentum of our social progress, and the vitality of the whole political environment. This environment can be rendered cold and barren by a citizenry fearful of political partisanship, by a public or a leadership that prefers to deal with labels and slogans rather than real problems and needs, or by a leadership too timid to venture from seemingly safe paths of the past.

The truth, in short, is that the federal idea—like the whole American experience—is a political adventure. It is no static thing, no dead definition, no dogmatic proclamation. Old as it is in our history, its secret strength is that it forever summons a free people to learn and try the new.

It requires us, I believe, to imitate its authors in only one respect: to be, like them, unchained to the past and unfearful of the future, to be—in our time as they were in theirs—political pioneers.

II

Federalism and National Life

The reports of the death of federalism, so authoritatively asserted in the nineteen-thirties, were, as we have seen, highly exaggerated. It serves little purpose, however, to dwell on the pitfalls of prediction. The task I have set for myself in this lecture is to examine the performance and the expanding promise of federalism in light of the hopes and aspirations of contemporary society for social progress, economic growth, and political stability. From this, I propose to develop, in this and the succeeding lecture, a still wider view of the federal idea—as indispensable not only to the solution of our domestic problems, but also—perhaps even more important—as indispensable to securing order and freedom for the free peoples of the international community.

If one examines the catalogue of hopes and fears before us today, there appears a striking

similarity to the list that confronted our countrymen in 1787 when the new Constitution, proposed
by the Philadelphia Convention, was submitted to
the thirteen states for ratification. What was the
dialogue between the voices in praise of and in
condemnation of the proposed federal frame of
government?

The fears were many, and they were stridently
expressed. In my own State of New York, in a
series of letters signed "Cato," Governor George
Clinton denounced the Constitution as being "as
inconsistent with the sovereign rights and powers
of the states as it would be of the civil rights and
liberties of the citizens." A North Carolina
preacher campaigning for election as a delegate
to the state ratification convention declared that
"the proposed Federal City would be a fortified
fortress of despotism." Elsewhere, critics attacked
the powers given to Congress by the new Constitution, contending that the hangman's noose
"would be among the mild instruments Congress
used to discipline." And one of the most frequently expressed criticisms of all was the brood-
ing fear that the new government would establish
a standing army "to enslave the people who will
be disarmed."

Any catalogue of these laments reveals that what
most bothered these early Americans were quite
specific fears: loss of sovereignty, arbitrary central

authority, loss of freedom of action, loss of control over their own destiny, and a domination of both people and government by provincial self-interest. This was an imposing list, and in light of their fresh recollections of oppression, none of these fears could be casually brushed aside.

Side by side with these fears, however, were the hopes of those patriots who perceived the far brighter side of the promise of American federalism under the new constitution. These were preeminently hopes for common security, for assuring personal freedom and protecting civil rights, for economic growth through a wider free-trade area and a common currency, and for social progress through the spread of education, cultural institutions, and other monuments of human progress without which no great civilizations can exist.

We all know, more or less well, the dramatic tale of how hope prevailed over fear in the launching of the American federal system. Yet, as André Gide remarked, ". . . you know the story. Nevertheless we will retell it. Everything has already been told; but as no one listens, we must always be beginning again."* Seldom in the long corridors of history can we find a better example of where the past can instruct the present.

* *The Return of the Prodigal, Preceded by Five Other Treatises, with Saul, a Drama in Five Acts,* tr. D. Bussy (London, 1953), p. 3.

In that remarkable document, *The Federalist,* which Jefferson called "the best commentary on the principles of government ever written," Hamilton, Madison, and Jay brilliantly marshalled the arguments for the hopes of the new government. The overriding mission of these men was to demonstrate in political practice that the "more perfect union" they envisioned would best serve the interests of their countrymen, and thus to expound a sweeping federalist idea beyond mere administrative federation.

This was a goal well outlined in the minds of many among the Founding Fathers, but for most of the people, it remained yet a matter of discovery, persuasion, and a need for unflagging leadership.

As we review the record after the passage of almost 175 years, the outstanding fact is that the federal framework of government, as it has evolved in the United States, has been a dramatic success.

The fears of those early Americans as they considered the new Constitution of 1787 for ratification have not materialized. The constitutional authority of the individual states today is undiminished. No arbitrary central authority has seized power, nor has provincialism crippled national policy. There has been no loss of freedom of action by the states nor of the people's control over their own destiny.

Rather the hopes of our forefathers have been realized, in some respects, beyond their wildest imaginings. The common security they sought has been maintained through seven wars from 1812 to Korea—including the terrible struggle of the Civil War in which the very life of the federal union was at issue. This nation's strength has not only tipped the scales in favor of freedom's cause in the two great world wars of this century: it has also been, for more than 16 years since World War II, the bulwark of freedom throughout the world.

Jefferson was convinced our federal system would nourish life, liberty, and the pursuit of happiness in an infant nation of less than four million people with an economy built around the small, independent farmer and shop proprietor. Yet this same fundamental political system today embraces and serves an economy that has achieved the widest distribution of individual earning power and wealth and the highest standard of living in recorded history. This is a nation producing 35 per cent of the world's goods through the organized effort of only 6 per cent of the world's population. Such economic growth has resulted not only from achievement of free trade among the states and adoption of a common currency, but also from a climate of economic freedom that has unleashed the dynamism and mobility, the inventiveness and the incentive, of free enterprise.

It is this economic growth, in turn, which has made possible achievement of the social, cultural, and educational goals our forefathers sought. For they succeeded in creating, in short, a federal system that, over the years, has proven flexible enough to foster both Hamilton's dream of modernized economic progress and Jefferson's passionate regard for the enhancement of individual freedom, opportunity, and responsibility. I think that Jefferson would indeed be pleased by the degree to which his values have been preserved in Hamilton's world.

Why has our federal system worked so well? Why has it been able to foster and adapt itself to fantastic growth and change over 175 years while preserving our fundamental human goals?

The answer lies in the nature of the federal idea and in the leadership which it summons. The truth is that in our federal system, the sources of productive power, initiative, and innovation are to be found at *all* levels of government, and they forever interact on each other, with the initiative depending importantly on where the most dynamic leadership exists. This means leadership with the vision to anticipate emerging problems and shape the forces behind them before they overwhelm us as crises.

As the needs and desires of peoples are perceived, in a federal system, they thus can be met as the opportunity, imagination, and energy of those who staff the multiple posts of power make it possible. At one time this may mean the thrust of wholly private initiative that matches a need with both action and ideas. As often, it will be an agency of state or local government that seizes the opportunity to serve. Or again—when the nation, as a whole, is moved by a condition not resolved by other public or private institutions—the national government can and will act with the necessary boldness and understanding.

There are many illustrations of this complex and productive sharing and yielding of power. Let us look, for example, at the persistent and fundamental concern of our people for civil rights.

It is significant that the Federal Constitution was approved by the states only when there was assurance that the first ten amendments designed to guarantee individual rights would be added. And most of the later amendments of substance have had similar purpose. Such basic guarantees in our society have enabled individual states to advance the granting of additional privileges and enhancement of civil liberties. Women's suffrage, for example, started in Wyoming in 1869, 51 years before the Nineteenth Amendment to the Federal Constitution. And such action by *one* state can create the issue and the pressure for action by other states and by the national government.

My own State of New York, I am happy to note, has been a pacesetter in effective legislation for individual opportunity and human rights. Over the years, it has pioneered in outlawing discrimination—based on race, creed, color, or national origin—in employment, education, public housing, multiple private housing, places of public assembly, and common carriers. Just last year we took action to close the final major gap with legislation outlawing discrimination in multiple private housing and commercial space—including discrimination by real estate brokers and mortgage institutions.

The power of the national government is available, and in many cases has been used, to resist state or local action which might deprive a person of basic civil rights. Thus in the nineteen-thirties it acted to assure freedom to read aloud the Declaration of Independence in Jersey City during the regime of Frank Hague. And more vivid and recent was the action to allow Negro students to attend the public schools in Little Rock.

There is still need, however, for more courageous leadership at the national level, both legislative and executive. For example, discrimination in federally financed housing could be eliminated by executive action alone.

Dual Sovereignty

The dual sovereignty of state and national governments has, thus, provided a practical method of meeting truly national problems without the establishment of an arbitrary central authority.

The sovereignty of the states, and their willingness to exercise it, stands as one of the principal barriers to the creation of a monolithic national bureaucracy that would stifle local initiative and regional creativity, and threaten liberty and opportunity. The local governments have no "sovereignty" to counterbalance federal sovereignty, nor the fiscal power to resist its blandishments. And this is a fact to be kept in mind when considering federal legislation in the areas of housing, social reform, urban renewal and the like, particularly if that legislation is designed to bypass the states.

Let me give you, from my own experience as governor, two different examples of how the willingness of a state to assert its sovereignty in the face of federal power has been productive of good for the people.

The first instance developed from legislation which I recommended to the Legislature, and which the people of New York State subsequently approved, providing a $75 million program to acquire land now for adequate park and recreation facilities, particularly in fast-growing metropolitan regions, before these facilities disappeared through development or became too expensive.

One particularly desirable site was owned by the federal government, which had declared it surplus. Acting under the preferential policy established for state and local governments to acquire such lands, our state representatives undertook negotiations. These negotiations, however, dragged on and on. There were differences as to market value, price, and for part of the property, appropriate use. Finally, federal officials decided to cut up the property into parcels and sell them to private parties. To save the land for park purposes, New York State took the position it would condemn the parcels for park purposes as soon as the federal government sold them. This proved a turning point in the negotiations. The state now owns the property and is developing it into a public park.

Atomic Energy

My second example is more dramatic—the asserting of state sovereignty in the field of atomic energy.

The national government once wholly monopolized this field, and, for military purposes, screened it in secrecy for more than a decade. Since 1954, private enterprise has been permitted by federal law to become active in this field, but it has not been able to mobilize sufficient resources to diminish significantly the federal government's effective monopoly in both research and development. As a result, the development and control of atomic energy has largely been isolated from the political and economic institutions closest to the people. These constricting circumstances have in many ways worked not only to the disadvantage of atomic development for the nation as a whole, but also to the detriment of the particular localities and regions that could benefit most from the free play of economic forces in this new and vital field.

This situation has been challenged and is being changed in New York. For the promotion of economic development and the protection of the public health and safety are critical and traditional responsibilities of states and localities. Early in 1959, we created an Office of Atomic Development to meet these responsibilities. This office has brought a new dimension to development of the atom for the peace-time needs and purposes of our state and nation.

Within a year following New York's action, and not unrelated to it, the Congress for the first time recognized and encouraged responsible state agencies to share the task of regulating atomic activities. More than this, we have created in New York a respected center to attract and stimulate new enterprises in atomic development, research and operations. We are now in the process of taking the next logical step.

The New York Legislature now has before it a proposal to create a State Atomic Research and Development Authority. By this Authority's ability to raise funds through public sale of bonds, it will for the first time sustain creative atomic development at a state and local level, with the stimulus it will bring to private research and industrial development. The Authority—if approved by the Legislature—will operate the state's new facility for processing and storing atomic industrial wastes. And it will launch such new explorations of the peaceful possibilities of atomic energy as a reactor for the testing of materials, a project for desalting sea water, and development of nuclear port facilities.

Thus have we been able to take the initiative in bringing this new energy to our state as a source of progress for our people in the fields of health, agriculture, and business. And the total social result will mean: new jobs, new products, new industries, and new knowledge.

To match this work on peaceful use of the atom, New York has pressed initiative—and prompted belated federal action—in a field supposedly an exclusive concern of the national government: the field of national defense.

No state responsibility is more fundamental than the protection of the health, the safety, and the well-being of each and every citizen. For lack of a truly serious effort at the national level, it is a fact that our people have been vulnerable and unprotected against the hazards of possible nuclear attack. In the absence of an effective national effort to meet this gravely serious state of affairs, it was left to the states and to the Governors' Conference to take the lead—by action, by example, and by advocacy—to create the awareness and the political tensions that only now, three years after the initial efforts, have led to a proposal for an effective national program to protect our people. This experience again strikingly demonstrates that, under a federal system, the states can take decisive initiative in any area where the needs of the people are truly perceived and truly involved.*

All these examples, drawn from divergent fields, illustrate the vitally important balance between state and national sovereignty within a federal system. To hold this vital balance, all of the states themselves must fully awaken to—and act on— their responsibilities and their opportunities. It is healthy, then, that there are movements under- way to remove the state constitutional, statutory, and administrative shackles that have prevented many states from playing their proper role. For if the states ignore or evade their responsibility to act in these areas, there will be alternative to direct federal-local action. If state inaction creates a vacuum, the federal government, under the pressure of public opinion, will fill it.

Even *without* state inaction, however, there is ever-present danger of direct federal-local action bypassing the states. And any such tendency would be a giant step toward unitary, monolithic govern-

* Equally significant is the fact that the very type and magni- tude of national action can be directly shaped by state leader- ship. In November of 1961, for example, the State of New York appropriated $100 million principally for encouragement of fallout-shelter construction near schools and colleges through- out the state, and in public buildings. It was not until after New York State launched this major effort that the President proposed a new federal program similar in type for the entire nation.

ment. The Kestenbaum Commission, appointed by President Eisenhower, stated the matter well: "The strengthening of State and local governments is essentially a task for the States themselves. . . . The success of our federal system thus depends in large measure upon the performance of the States."*

My own initiation to state government was as chairman of the State Constitutional Revision Commission. One of my first acts as Governor was to initiate the first comprehensive reorganization of the executive branch of the New York state government since the pioneering reorganization of Governor Alfred E. Smith nearly 40 years ago. To date we have passed one constitutional amendment and 45 statutes reorganizing the executive branch of New York state government, as well as a constitutional amendment providing for the first reorganization of our New York state-court system in 115 years.

Federal Grants-in-Aid

One of the major factors in preserving the balance in the federal system—and averting the growth of arbitrary central authority, while meeting essential social and economic needs requiring

* *The Commission on Intergovernmental Relations: A Report to the President for Transmittal to the Congress* (June 1955), pp. 36, 37.

federal participation—has been the federal program of grants-in-aid to the states.

Grants-in-aids first appeared in modern form in 1879. Ever since, they have made it possible to draw upon the huge fiscal resources of the federal government to meet urgent needs without direct national administration of the programs. By the last year of the Hoover administration, federal expenditures under grant-in-aid legislation totalled over $200 million. With the great surge of federal aid under the New Deal, with postwar inflation and with new postwar programs, federal grants-in-aid had climbed to $2.3 billion by 1952. The value and need of such programs, however, have been recognized by both our national parties—as indicated by the fact that, by the end of the Eisenhower administration, their sum had risen to an annual $7.3 billion, principally as a result of a major expansion of the federal interstate highway program.

Rather than promote arbitrary central authority, the grant-in-aid has served to strengthen the weaker states fiscally, to equalize opportunity for participation in social programs, and to establish certain minimum standards of performance. A state like Wyoming draws almost one-third of its budget from such grants. The comparable figure for New York State is barely eight per cent.

State Grants-in-Aid

Again, in the spirit of our federal system, state governments, in order to preserve and advance the vitality and strength of local governments, have themselves given grants-in-aid to equalize opportunity and assist in the financing of education, highways, and social programs. Today this New York State aid to localities reaches a sum six times the size of such federal aid. This has enabled local governments to continue to administer services close to the people, frequently on a scale beyond the limited fiscal capacities of many local communities.

The budget which I have just submitted to the New York State Legislature, for example, allocated $1,381,000,000 for local assistance purposes in the form of state grants-in-aid. This is about 51 per cent of a budget totalling some $2.6 billion. Some idea of the growth of state aid can be gauged when one notes that in this budget, some $908 million is for aid to education—as against $569 million when I took office three years ago. In other words the State Legislature and I will have added $85 million per year for four successive years in aid to education.

The abiding importance of all such federal devices and procedures—evolving over the decades since the adoption of the United States Constitution—has been to help meet and dispel all initial fears that the people would lose control over their own destiny. Innumerable other measures have helped to secure that control. Suffrage has been vastly extended. Democratic procedures like the secret ballot, direct primaries, and popular election of United States Senators have been instituted.

The federal government thus has not become an uncontrollable colossus, and over the years the nation's Congress has been a bulwark of the federal system—its membership, and the political parties represented within it, alike being state-based. This is not to say that the Congress does not look beyond local interests to national and international ones, but it does provide an ever-present voice for state and local concerns within the framework of the national government itself. As Governor, I recognized early in my administration the importance of close cooperation with New York State's 45-member Congressional delegation. We have met periodically on a nonpartisan basis. A steering committee of the Congressional delegation, chaired by a senior member of the House of Representatives—a Democrat, by the way—is in continuing communication with the state administration in furthering state programs and interests.

The Urban Challenge to the Federal Idea

There is no greater challenge in our age to the inventiveness of the federal idea than the surging tide of urbanism. And here—while all three levels of government in the United States are necessarily involved—the states have a crucial role. Regrettably, they are only now coming to recognize it.

The problems of urbanism have outrun individual local government boundaries, legal powers, and fiscal resources. And the national government is too remote to sense and to act responsively on the widely varying local or regional concerns and aspirations. The states—through their relations with local governments, their greater resources and powers, and their closeness to the people and the problems—can and should serve as the leaders in planning, and the catalysts in developing, cooperative action at local-state-federal levels.

During the last three years, we have been working to adapt the structure of New York State government to meet the requirements of urbanism. Three new offices have been created—an Office for Local Government, an Office of Transportation, and an Office for Urban and Regional Development.

The Office for Local Government serves as a clearing house for information and provides technical assistance for counties, cities, towns, villages,

and special districts. In its brief three-year life-
time, it has served well in stimulating and facili-
tating interlocal cooperation. As a result of the
activities of this office, comprehensive legislation
has been enacted creating a framework within
which local governments can plan and work together.

The Office of Transportation has concentrated
its attention and efforts in the long neglected area
of commuter rail service and other metropolitan
transportation problems. This office, in cooperation with the Port of New York Authority, admin-
isters the state's new $100 million commuter-car
program, while also conducting a series of transportation planning and cost studies.

The Office for Urban and Regional Development serves to coordinate the work of our own
state departments and agencies—conservation,
parks, highways and public works, housing and
urban renewal, commerce and transportation. And
it strives to relate these state activities to plans
and programs on three other levels: local, regional,
and federal.

Apart from these coordinating agencies, the
state is undertaking large-scale substantive programs to meet directly the growing problems of
urban life. In the field of low-rent housing, New
York has been a pioneer. It entered the field in

1926, well before the federal government. Now, in recent years, the state has pioneered in the particular sphere of middle-income housing. The magnitude of the problem in this sphere is clearly illustrated by the fact that in 1959, when I took office, 45 per cent of New York City's population fell in the middle-income bracket, and yet only 12 per cent of the housing being built was in the middle-income range.

Since I have been governor, I have been trying to solve the problem of how to tap the sources of private capital to greatly expand the privately sponsored middle-income housing program. This past year a major break-through was achieved with creation of the State Housing Finance Agency as a vehicle for the financing of limited-profit, middle-income housing with 90 per cent loans to private builders. The agency has an authorized capital of over $500 million which it raises by the sale of bonds to private investors with its mortgages as security. In less than a year, it has already committed $237 million for housing projects under private ownership.

In similar ways, the challenge of urban problems across the nation is being met with state and local public-works projects which stagger the imagination in size and scope. The State of California has just approved a $2 billion bond issue for water supply. New York State is completing a thruway costing over $1 billion.

Interstate Cooperation

All these massive problems of urbanism also pose new challenges for cooperation *between* and *among* the states, as well as for local-state-federal cooperation. And although there are striking examples of interstate cooperation, the potentialities for cooperative action in this area are virtually untapped. For interstate action can at times obviate the need for federal action, and interstate action with federal participation in regional problems is only in its early infancy.

New York and New Jersey, through the Port of New York Authority, have successfully worked together some 40 years to develop their joint port areas, including operation of toll bridges and tunnels between the two states. The two states are also directing the Port Authority to undertake a $350 million project to construct a World Trade Center in lower Manhattan, and to take over the bankrupt Hudson and Manhattan railroad, a crucial commuter facility running between northern New Jersey and New York City. This will represent the first time in our country, to my knowledge, that the proceeds from automobile toll facilities will be helping to finance commuter

rail transportation. And this same bi-state Authority is also planning a fourth major airport for the
New York Port area—at an estimated cost of
more than $300 million.

Such potentialities of interstate cooperation
have further been dramatically illustrated in the
four-state effort to keep the New Haven Railway
in operation. In August of 1960, when the critical
situation of that railroad was brought to our attention, I joined with the Governors of Massachusetts, Connecticut, and Rhode Island in
establishing the Interstate Staff Committee on the
New Haven. This committee has been at work
ever since and has developed an interim plan to
assure the railroad's operation until a long-range
solution could be developed. In an unprecedented
example of joint state action, the four states have
passed legislation to eliminate $6.2 million an-
nually in taxes from the railroad, thus virtually
freeing this railroad from all real-property taxes.
Passenger fares were raised ten per cent and, in
New York State, local governments were authorized to take over passenger station maintenance.
Unfortunately, the federal government has not
yet eliminated the ten per cent passenger excise
tax, and the recommended labor-management
savings have not been achieved.

Joint Interstate and Federal Action

To meet regional problems satisfactorily, however, there is real need for much more cooperative planning and action between the states and the federal government.

The New Haven Railway—again—is a case in point. This is an interstate railroad under federal jurisdiction, a vital artery for interstate commerce and national defense. Since interstate action alone cannot guarantee the railroad's continuance, the interested governors have requested the President to name a representative to the Interstate Staff Committee and to establish a focal point in the federal government with which we could work to resolve the railroad's problems.

We also have urged upon the President the establishment of a transportation policy for the United States. Unless there is a national transportation policy established by the only government with the authority to set one, there is no satisfactory framework within which the states, either individually or together, can act on matters like the New Haven railroad or the large number of railroad mergers, consolidations, and control proposals now pending.

Another promising and pioneering effort at joint interstate and federal action is the recently-created Delaware River Basin Commission. Here the Governors of four states—Delaware, Pennsylvania, New Jersey, and New York—sit with a single representative of the federal government appointed by the President as the governing board of an agency to plan and develop the water resources of the Delaware River basin.

And yet a third such example is the Tri-State Transportation Committee established in August of 1961 by the Governors of New Jersey, Connecticut, and New York to deal with transportation problems and their relation to land-use patterns of the New York metropolitan region. The federal government was invited to have representation on the committee, and we are pleased that the United States Bureau of Public Roads and the Housing and Home Finance Agency have been actively participating through their representatives.

These three instances of new action have one important quality in common: in all three, it was the *states* that took the initiative. Again, we are strikingly reminded of the limitless creative potential in the federal idea—if it be but clearly seen and courageously applied.

———

I have drawn these explicit examples—from the political laboratory of state government—to suggest the range and variety of challenges that invite state initiative within the federal system. I believe they dramatically prove that this is no time for states to mourn a lack of challenges—or a lack of the power to meet them.

The essential political truth is that—today more than ever—the preservation of states' rights depends upon the exercise of states' responsibilities. We stand, in fact, upon the threshold of a new test of leadership at the state level. For—so great and urgent are the demands of national defense and foreign policy upon all resources of the national government—that, now as never in our history, state governments are challenged to face and meet the pressing *domestic* concerns of our society.

This, then, can prove to be an historic moment in the long evolution of our federal idea. For it summons us to remember and to apply a basic fact of American political history—the fact that our states are designed to be our great centers for political experiment. This—as Lord Bryce discerned long ago—is perhaps the key role of the state: to be the proving ground for ever new ventures in free government. The crisis of the nineteen-thirties impelled too many of us to forget all this. As national government was hailed to be the source of great political initiative, the state governments tended to fall back into a defensive posture. They showed themselves fretfully concerned with rights, rather than boldly concerned with responsibilities.

The time is upon us now to assert again the older and more vital tradition—to call upon our states to be active where they have been passive —progressive where they have been timid—creative where they have been merely cautious. In a word, it is time for the states to—*lead*.

This makes good history, good politics, and good sense. But it signifies something still more meaningful. It can help to make America, in the eyes of a world watching and wondering about the fate of freedom itself, a living proof of the ability of free men to govern themselves in ways forever new, inventive, and inspiring. And thus it can help the nation to fill its role of leadership among the free peoples of the world.

It is, then, an historic challenge. In its full sweep, it requires us, as Americans, to do two things. It invites us to look to our past—inward, upon our own national experience with the federal idea. And it summons us to look to our future— outward, in a vision that can embrace the destiny of all free peoples.

We see, as we look upon our own past, beginning with our birth as a nation, the historic host of achievements so closely bound to our own practice of the federal idea . . . the blending of thirteen separate sovreignties into a federal union that would bring civil order and peace—to a whole continent . . . the national commitment to the principle of personal freedom, so that all political power has been defined, limited and directed to serve—and never to suppress—the people . . . the liberation of the creative energies of a free economy, made possible by a political framework of order encouraging individual initiative, providing a common currency, and widening the area of free trade and commerce . . . the unmatched pace of scientific and technological advance, propelled both by individual imagination and capital accumulation . . . the constant—not always swift, but never forgotten—struggle to assure civil rights and liberties to all citizens . . . a struggle that once carried us as a people into the chasm of civil strife . . . and a struggle that, even as it scores new gains each decade and year, still demands proof, forever fresh and new, of our faith in the dignity of man . . . the struggle, too, across the whole front of social progress, as we have sought to give all men an essential measure of human and social security, to extend to all equal opportunity, and to widen constantly the range of this opportunity—for the well-being of all, the self-fulfillment of each.

All these are great and memorable attainments for a people. We can and do take pride in them. And we can recognize and respect the role, in their achievement, that belongs to the federal idea. Yet —when we look outward upon this world of the midtwentieth century—we must face the clear challenge of a paradox. All the triumphs of our own national life still do not assure even our national security in the world we live in. We see, then, that all the monuments of the past are matched—in number and in greatness—by the menaces of the present.

There is the lack of even simple safety that we —or any nation, however mighty or healthy—can enjoy in solitude.

There is the inexorable need of all free peoples to devise new formulas of unity—for their physical security, their political stability, their economic progress . . . a need quite as compelling as that which required this union of colonies into a new nation almost two centuries ago.

There are the impediments to economic growth in a world of free peoples lacking political unity or stability—the tariff walls choking off channels of trade, the artificial shielding behind these walls of uneconomic industries, the towering difficulties of capital accumulation in new-born nations, and the virtual impossibility of free economic initiative in a political world of uncertainty and upheaval.

There is the threat that even such political bonds as do exist, among free peoples, may be sundered by the claims and rigors of quickening economic competition—as great powers clash in conflict for markets too narrow to admit all.

And there is the constant, unrelenting menace of a Communist Imperialism—eager to divide all free nations, prompt to fill all political vacuums, ready with its own rude version of a world order.

All these factors write their warning message to free nations in letters tall and bold enough for all to read. It says simply: the attempt of any free nation today to stand alone—or its refusal to strive toward new and larger unity with other free peoples—conveys no more sense or realism, hope or promise, than for a Massachusetts or a New York to try to pit itself against such challenges and such forces. Thus are we led—by our own experience as a people and as a nation—to turn and face the *world,* and boldly seek the answer to the question: how can all free peoples, so fatefully bound together in this twentieth century, attain such unity and strength as free men of the eighteenth century built upon this land of ours?

III

Federalism and Free World Order

I dedicate this final lecture to one basic proposition. It is this: the federal idea, which our Founding Fathers applied in their historic act of political creation in the eighteenth century, can be applied in this twentieth century in the larger context of the world of free nations—if we will but match our forefathers in courage and vision. The first historic instance secured freedom and order to this new nation. The second can decisively serve to guard freedom and to promote order in a free world. Sweeping as this assertion may be, I believe it to be anything but an academic proposition. Quite the contrary: it is a matter of cold political realism.

For the realities before us—the erosion of world order and the peril to world freedom—present challenges of a size and greatness never before known. They cannot be met by defensive devices, mere tactical maneuvers, or the most cunningly contrived improvisation. Political creation, not improvisation, is the order of the day. And anything less than a grand design—a major idea and a lofty sense of purpose—is too puny for the time in which we live.

Even at much earlier times in our national history, the world scene stirred many in America to ponder the problems of world peace. More than a century ago, late in the eighteen-forties, one such group of concerned citizens was joined by Ralph Waldo Emerson. He journeyed out to the Middle West to meet with kindred spirits gathered there in sober conclave to discuss the structure of a world organization. After long days of debate on both the nature of such a sovereignty and its physical location, it was decided that the future seat of world order would be Constantinople. With this, Emerson's patience snapped, and he stalked from the conference, exclaiming with splendid New England disdain: "It's too far from Concord."

Ours indeed is a fantastically different world. It is a world in which all distances are shrivelled, all great perils universal, and the great globe itself is hardly more than a neighborhood. It is a world divided by a fundamental and basic conflict— underlying all the military, economic, and political tensions of our times. This conflict finds—on one side—those who, believing in the dignity and worth of the individual, proclaim his right to be free to achieve his full destiny—spiritually, intellectually, and materially. And—on the other side—there are arrayed those who, denying and disdaining the worth of the individual, subject him to the will of an authoritarian state, the dictates of a rigid ideology, and the ruthless disciplines of a party apparatus.

This basic conflict—so deeply dividing the world—comes at a time when the surge of other changes and upheavals staggers the mind and senses. Whole nations are trying to vault from the Stone Age to the twentieth century. Other nations are trying, no less audaciously, to hurl themselves to the moon.

All the while, all free peoples—from the United States to Togoland, from Brazil to Pakistan, from Italy to India—grapple at home with hopes and fears, challenges and dangers, as deep and meaningful for our times as those confronting the first American colonists. These hopes and fears are bound up in problems as fundamental as food and shelter for an exploding population—and as complex as the interlocking factors of unemployment, automation, and productivity.

From the most remote farm to the most sprawling urban centers, the problems and crises in housing and transportation, education and health, mark a world of hope but insecurity, of opportunity yet disparity. We groan under crop surpluses —produced by eight per cent of our population, in a world of hungry millions. Yet the hungry are exploited by the propaganda of a Communist system unable to produce enough food—even with more than 50 per cent of its people at work on its farms from dawn to dusk seven days a week.

Of all times in our history, this would be the most inconceivable in which to dismiss or to disparage any truly creative political concept as too bold or too large to meet the challenges of the hour.

———————

We are living in an age when (in the words of Walter Prescott Webb) we "look down the long gun-barrel of history."* At such a time our sights and all our perceptions and faculties must be set for new ideas. For the problems—of defense and commerce, of surplus and shortage—are simply outrunning the political mechanisms for handling them.

The essence of the global crisis of this mid-twentieth century is the urgent need and quest, in the world of free nations, for the answer to this

* *The Southwest Review* 34 (1949), 329.

question: how can free men guard and foster freedom, diversity, and progress within a framework of order and unity? The free world, in short, is grappling with precisely the political equation—the elements of order and the factors of freedom—whose balancing has been the supreme political achievement of our nation's history.

Since World War II, we have obviously looked beyond the purely national horizon of this attainment to our new role in the world. In this role, we have done much to recognize our military responsibility in the cause of freedom. We have also done much to employ our economic power as an essential source of strength and progress for all free nations. We have failed, however, to face up to the fundamental political problem—the creation of a free world structure of order and unity.

What we must do is to provide that political leadership essential to build a framework within which the basic and urgent aspirations of free men and free nations can be realized. And we can begin this historic task by recognizing the political relevance of the federal idea to the destiny of the free world as a whole. This, I believe, quickly becomes clear from a review of the deterioration of the structures for political order in the world.

Let us look at a few plain facts.

First: No nation today can defend its freedom, or

fulfill the needs and aspirations of its own people, from within its own borders or through its own resources alone. No nation today can accelerate growth and industrialization to provide more jobs and higher living standards for a growing population—apart from other nations, their development and their trade. Military defense, economic growth, rising living standards, widening opportunities for individual fulfillment—all these prime essentials of modern life for free men require the joint and co-operative action of many sovereignties. And so the nation-state, standing alone, threatens, in many ways, to seem as anachronistic as the Greek city-state eventually became in ancient times.

Second: The old patterns and formulas of international order have been shattered. The European empires, whatever their iniquities, did provide frameworks within which diverse and distant peoples could live and work together. Today, virtually all these structures have disintegrated—leaving an historic political vacuum.

Third: The United Nations, repository of so much hope, has not been able—nor can it be able —to shape a new world order as events now so compellingly command. The structure of the UN is such that it can function effectively only when there is essential agreement on purpose and procedure, among the five permanent members of the Security Council. But the Communist bloc has dedicated itself to the manipulation of the UN's democratic processes, so astutely and determinedly, as largely to frustrate its intended power and role. As a result, the UN lacks the strength to master or control the forces that it confronts.

The enduring value of the UN, nonetheless, remains three-fold: as the universal symbol of humanity's hopes for peace, as a forum for voicing and hearing all the divisions and basic conflicts that imperil these hopes, and as a channel for daily communication between nations.

Fourth: The ultimate challenge of Communist imperialism is its promise to fill the political vacuum in world order created by the collapse of old empires and the failure of anything else to take their place. Such a vacuum is as abhorrent to politics as to nature. And Communism offers a design—a cruel design—for world order.

The Communists have done their best, of course, to divide the free peoples of the world and to thwart the creation of the new political methods and instruments for securing order, peace, and freedom. But the true thrust of Communism far surpasses the mere making of menacing, scornful gestures against the old order already crumbling —or a new and free order struggling to be born.

It seeks to create the illusion that a Communist world order will be more secure, more rational, and more geared to the realities of modern life, science, and technology than any other structure, past or present.

This Communist new order itself, incidentally, is based on a *false* federalism whose pattern may be found in the Soviet Union itself. The Union of Soviet Socialist Republics has outward signs of a federalist structure—as its very name implies. But here, as elsewhere, the Communists have merely taken our words, our forms, our very symbols of man's hopes and aspirations and have corrupted them to mislead and to deceive in their quest for world domination. Stalin, in fact, used to boast of the wonderful federal government established by the Soviet Constitution of 1936. But it was quickly apparent that federalism in the Soviet sense did not go beyond the sterile pages of the document itself—while the actual practice of Soviet government was a kind of pitiless central-ism that completely disregarded the nation's own proclaimed fundamental laws. Instead of a shared sovereignty flowing from the people, instead of the dynamic interplay of competitive political parties, free economic enterprise and voluntary social ef-fort, all matters—political, economic and social—are met, of course, by the iron rule of one party from Moscow. It therefore is not surprising that no free nation has ever gone Communist of its own volition and the rule of Communism has always had to be imposed by political coups with military backing.

Fifth: It is a tragic fact that the free world today offers no secure structure of international order within which the basic aspirations of free men may be realized, and the safety and rights of free nations be guarded. And the rush of events has ironically compounded the problem. Just as the nation-state is becoming less and less competent to perform its international political tasks, the number of such states has been increasing with a speed unmatched in history.

Glance, for a moment, at the wreckage around us—the wreckage of political concepts that still seemed coherent and alive in the first part of this century. Even by the interwar period of the thirties both statesmen and historians were caustically appraising what scholars have called the "absurd architecture" of the world.* Since World War II, along with the scientific revolution and the advent of nuclear power, the "absurdity" of 30 years ago borders on farce, if not chaos—as the fever of nationalism has swept across Asia and Africa. Peo-

* Herbert Agar, *The City of Man: A Declaration on World Democracy* (New York, 1941), p. 27.

ple after people—passionately and understandably
eager to set their own destinies—inevitably have
turned to the nation-state, so ill-equipped, standing alone, to meet the twentieth century's great
challenges.

Within these new-born nations, a host of additional factors conspire to threaten instability and
disorder. In some instances, these nations' boundaries reflect nothing more than the accidents of
past colonial rivalries. In other cases, regional or
tribal internal divisions threaten their newly proclaimed unity. Almost all these nations suffer
acutely from lack of political leadership trained
for the most elementary tasks of governing. They
lack a political party system basic to preserving the
vital forces of democracy. And with passionate
ardor, all of these nations seek to achieve, in a few
swift years, an economic transformation that older
Western nations spent centuries to attain and that
can never come without securing true political
stability.

Such is the size of the matters before us. And
all these problems are exacerbated by the astute-
ness and implacability of the Communist con-
spiracy, with its tireless genius for crisis.

The historic choice fast rushing upon us, then,
is no less than this: either the free nations of the
world will take the lead in adapting the federal

concept to their relations, or, one by one, we may be driven into the retreat of the perilous isolationism—political, economic, and intellectual—so ardently sought by the Soviet policy of divide-and-conquer.

These are the facts of life that free men must face. They constitute a challenge that would essentially be just as profound and urgent if there were no Communist menace to torment free peoples anywhere on earth.

This challenge is: how can free nations design a political structure for their world in which free men can enjoy a life that will respect the dignity of the individual and allow them to work out their own destinies, realize their national aspirations, enhance their opportunities for progress, and join with their neighbors in a society secure from violence and assault?

This is the question that today tests and summons all our political creativity, imagination, and courage.

—————

I believe, as I have said, that the answer to the historic problems the free world confronts can be found in the federal idea. I am not speaking of panaceas or slogans, nor of fanciful blueprints or meticulous (and meaningless) charts. I am speaking of a direction in which free men can begin to think, to act, and—in the case of the United States particularly—to lead.

As we have faced some of the urgent challenges of the period since World War II, we have taken some important and well-known actions in the military, economic, and political fields. Many of these steps meant major breaks with the traditions of the past. Yet they all have been, at best, only fragmentary and partial efforts, generally sparked by sudden and isolated crises. They have not been integral parts of a coherent structure of international order, conceived and created to forestall crises.

Everywhere now the political bills are coming due—as we are called to pay the price for years of mere improvisation.

In Latin America, one glance suffices to make the sad reckoning. Years have been wasted—in neglect of all chances to lead boldly toward continental unity. Now we find ourselves, in many ways, a hemisphere divided.

In Western Europe, the very durability of our alliance has come now to depend critically on devising new formulas for planning nuclear defense. The great Western European nations cannot be expected to live indefinitely in a state of essential dependence on the United States' decision to use, or not to use, its nuclear deterrent. Obviously, the need is for more cohesive political unity to govern the common defense.

The truths and needs thus so clear in military and political spheres are equally plain and urgent in *economic* affairs. In Europe, the Common Market has been a concept fostered and propagated by the United States for more than a decade. Now that it is here and prospering, we must define our relation to the old world in view of this new economic power. Ancient fears of growing foreign competition will make this, in all probability, the major issue of national debate for the current year.

While the Latin American Free Trade Area, the GATT organization, and various commodity trade agreements throughout the free world are all moving to open the channels of trade, still it has been impossible to create the framework of order needed to unleash the creative possibilities of free enterprise as an economic catalyst in the free world.

Let me dwell on this matter—with great emphasis. Here—with this blunting and stifling of the creative energy of free enterprise—we pay one of the heaviest prices for our failure to achieve a structure for international order. Our fragmentary approach has not given free-enterprise capitalism a chance to serve the needs of the people of the free world as it has in the United States. Here, a free-enterprise capitalism within a federal system has produced the world's highest standard of living with the widest distribution of income. Yet for the industrial nations of the free world to share the benefits of this system in any meaningful sense requires, above all, an international climate of political stability.

We should recognize more clearly that the private sector is of crucial importance to the process of successful economic development in democratic societies. We have tried to make up for a lack of the dynamic, creative economic force of private initiative, technology, and capital in the less-developed areas by an elaborate system of United States government-to-government foreign aid. Useful as this has been, it has not provided the economic dynamism and drive needed to increase production, raise standards of living, and improve social conditions at a rate even comparable to the population growth of many of these nations.

In the United States, the management of productive activity is more than 90 per cent private, but it is less generally recognized that such activity in most of the newly developed areas is also in private hands. For one thing, agricultural and pastoral activities bulk very large in almost all of these areas. At the same time a large share of the expenditures of their governments for construction of power projects, transport and communication facilities, irrigation projects, schools, hospitals, and housing developments are contracted for with private firms. Thus the pace of development that these countries seek could not be attained merely by expansion of the relatively small fraction of activities conducted under government auspices alone.

These developing nations, not yet able to generate internally sufficient investment funds for economic expansion, suffer from the absence of a free world political structure that would encourage the free flow of such funds along with the technical knowledge and management skills that accompany them. Obviously, the degree of private investment, foreign or domestic, attracted to the fields for which it is best adapted—manufacturing, extractive, commercial, and personal services— will determine the availability of scant government funds for such public necessities as dams, roads, schools, and hospitals.

The need, therefore, is urgent to harness the unparalleled resources of free enterprise to the task of meeting human needs and aspirations throughout the free world. Nor does this deny that contracts for public services—as in agriculture, education, and public health—could continue to be on a government-to-government basis or in terms of a combination of government and private philanthropic undertakings. For we must remember that in this country there is a free enterprise of philanthropy and voluntary service as well as a free enterprise based on profit and loss.

All these, then, are some of the reasons—economic, military, political—pressing us to lead vigorously toward the true building of a new world order. And it urgently requires, I believe, that the United States take the leadership among all free peoples to make the underlying concepts and aspirations of national sovereignty truly meaningful through the federal approach.

———

How does the federal idea evolve and apply in the future immediately before us? Let us look again at the crucial economic and political facts of life. They show problems assailing *all* free nations.

Here in the United States we are enjoying a period of prosperity—yet we also are living in serious fear of the economic competition of our friends and the intercontinental missiles of potential enemies. Free West Germany booms, but

Communist East Germany is hungry, and Berlin
—the city divided—symbolizes the nation divided.
Across the globe, Japan, too, is booming—and
vulnerable. Her postwar economic growth has
been fabulous, and her trade reaches to all corners
of the globe; but her overcrowded population, her
need for expanding markets, and the aggressive
nature of her Communist neighbors threaten
grave future troubles.

And so it goes throughout the free world—
whether in industrial nations such as England,
Germany, Japan, and the United States; whether
in industrializing nations still heavily tied to their
agricultural economies, such as in Brazil or India;
whether in newly emerging nations like Nigeria
or the Sudan. Everywhere we see free nations in
suspense—in midpassage—in danger. Yet—matching their fears—are their hopes and their capacities for a far better life.

All the problems we face have this in common:
we cannot solve one of them in isolation. And in
their basic nature these problems are strikingly
similar to those faced by the original 13 American
colonies—problems of security and of trade, of
growth and of order, and above all, the human
aspirations of the free individual.

I have long felt that the road toward the unity
of free nations lay through regional confederations

—in the Western Hemisphere and in the Atlantic community, perhaps eventually in Africa, the Middle East, and Asia. Such work toward regional unities is, in fact, steadily progressing. The Common Market in Europe is an outstanding example. These developments are hopeful and may prove historic.

But events in the world are moving with such swiftness—and the danger to the free world is so great—that increasingly I believe that our advances toward unity must now extend to action *between* regions as well as *within* them. Moreover, some problems before us may well be capable of solution only within a political framework larger than simple regionalism. I think, for one example, of the political situation here in this Western Hemisphere. The political front against Castro is a shaky one, indeed. And the trade ties of Latin republics with England, Germany, Japan and other nations conflict with hemisphere free-trade aims.

Elsewhere in the great regions of the world, we see political chaos in Africa for which there appears to be no African solution, Arab-Israeli division running too deep to be settled in a Middle Eastern context alone, Asia split three ways—by Communism, by neutralism, and by commitment to the West. In Europe, too, while the moves toward political collaboration within the Common Market lend great encouragement to hopes for eventual free-world unity, nonetheless the present benefits of the Common Market are limited primarily to its members—and those outside it have a fierce competitor to face.

I was wholeheartedly committed to the battle at the San Francisco Conference in 1945 for inclusion of Article 51 in the United Nations Charter to permit regional arrangements within the UN framework. And I certainly do not now abandon my belief in the value and importance of regional arrangements among free nations. But I have come to the conviction that events are driving us rapidly beyond even the limits of regional concepts—to the logic of applying the federal idea wherever possible, among free nations however distant, however seemingly strong in themselves.

For the force and value of the federal idea are not limited to the small, newer, weaker nations. The need is just as great for the most traditionally powerful. The very passing of the structure of old world empires has underscored the historic necessity dramatically. Their own trade and commerce with one another, as well as with the smaller nations, and the greater political unity of the free world, will decisively determine if they are to stay strong and free.

What our common danger and our common aspirations imperatively require, then, is a common commitment to some basic principles and purposes—to all those traditions, laws, and principles assuring the freedom of the individual; to the need for larger unity to assure common defense; to the necessity of removing barriers to commerce; and ultimately to the gradual devising of political forms of unity.

I suggest to you that the federal experience within this nation is directly pertinent to all these great challenges before the world community. Let me give you some specific examples . . .

Just as no city or county or state within our Federal Union can live unto itself and meet its problems, so is it equally impossible for any nation—even the strongest nation—to secure its own freedom by its own resources.

Just as the operation of our own national economy and social life is interdependent with a federal system of government, assuring freedom and order, so just as dramatically do the economic and social workings of a free economy in the world require movement toward a federal idea, bringing order to the chaos of nation-states.

The very social and economic problems that require political action and leadership on the most close-to-home levels of local American government—problems of education, transportation, power resources, economic growth—are the *same* problems that challenge action by nations large and small in all regions of the earth.

Just as the equalization principle within our own nation recognizes that an Arkansas or a Tennessee can meet its economic problems only within a larger political framework, so the same basic concept of federalism applies on the world scene to the economic problems of a Bolivia or a Burma.

Just as the American federal system invites the larger and stronger states to take the lead in showing the nation new political paths, so should this nation as a whole, along with all the more powerful free nations, assume a similar role of leadership in the world at large.

These, I think, are sufficient ways to suggest that the American experience with federalism has meaning for the world.

More specifically, I hope and urge:

First: that we develop an understanding at home of the nature and character of the problems that we and the other free nations face—and the significance of the federal idea as a practical framework within which they can be solved.

Second: That leaders throughout the free world work to develop a consensus of purpose and bring forth positive suggestions and recommendations for practical application of the federal idea to the problems before us all.

Third: That informal, intergovernmental consultations by the political leaders of free nations be undertaken to define agreed objectives and develop means to achieve them through application of the federal idea.

Fourth: That these consultations be supplemented by regional and functional conferences to attack specific problems and launch explicit programs.

Out of this, I would venture to prophesy that —sooner perhaps than we may realize and despite the enormity of the apparent difficulties—there will evolve the bases for a federal structure of the free world.

In this year of 1962, these may seem visionary concepts. In the year 1787, similar doubts and fears surged up. And they, too, turned on such words as sovereignty, centralism, restriction.

To all who find cause for alarm—or scorn—in such sweeping concepts as these, I would commend a remembrance of some words written early in our nation's life. "Hearken not," it was written, "to the voice which petulantly tells you that the form of government recommended for your adoption is a novelty in the political world; that it has never yet had a place in the theories of the wildest projectors; that it rashly attempts what it is impossible to accomplish. No, my countrymen, shut your ears against this unhallowed language."*

These were the words of that dedicated Federalist, James Madison. And the political formula he was defending—against widespread charges of brash and reckless innovation—was the Constitution of the United States.

In essence, the answer of Madison and the other Federalists to these cries of scorn was this: there is no other way to bring order and to assure freedom on this continent. I believe that the vitality of the federal idea is such that precisely the same statement is equally true today of the world of free peoples.

The words of Lord Bryce**—spoken in the first Godkin lecture in 1904—never held greater meaning than at this moment in our history. "All of you are at times fascinated by a dream of this country as it might be," he said. "The citizen of the United States should keep ever before him the splendid vision of a great republic, not only prosperous, but pure and happy, and working only for the good of her people. No other country

* *The Federalist*, ed. J. E. Cooke (Cleveland and New York, 1961), p. 88.
** The *Boston Evening Transcript*, November 4, 1904.

has had similar opportunities . . . such immunity from old evils, to start with. On the success of the United States in working free government wisely and well, more than upon that of any other country, the future of mankind depends." And he concluded: "May the generation that is now rising throw themselves into this glorious enterprise for the benefit of the entire world. . . ."

There is one final reason for seeing the United States in such a role, and it is deeper than all others, practical or philosophic. It is the fact that our dominant commitment from our very birth as a nation has been to everlasting concern for the individual, his freedom and his dignity.

This is why we were born as a nation—not as an economic convenience or as an imperial adventure. We came into being for the sake of an *idea:* our belief that man should be free to fulfill his unique and individual destiny—a belief based upon our dedicated faith in the brotherhood of all mankind. The nation that was founded in the eighteenth century provided a home—a political structure—in which free men could live a life of such fulfillment.

Yet this, in a real sense, could never be enough. No matter how this nation strove to isolate itself in past generations, it could never suppress or deny an impulse toward the world. In one age, this impulse expressed itself through missionaries; in another age, through philanthropy, medical care, deeds of charity; and most recently, through massive international aid and assistance.

There is a reason why this impulse has always asserted itself. Our Founding Fathers, obviously, built a home for one nation. Yet the idea to which they and this nation were committed—the idea of human freedom—was, is, and can *only* be universal.

We are bound as a people, in the deepest sense, to live by this commitment with a boldness, a confidence, and a clarity of vision matching those who led this nation to life.